Luna Moth

Written By
Laura Appleton-Smith

Illustrated By
Carol Vredenburgh

Laura Appleton-Smith holds a degree in English from Middlebury College.
Laura is a primary school teacher who has combined her talents in creative writing with
her experience in early childhood education to create *Books to Remember*.
She lives in New Hampshire with her husband, Terry.

Carol Vredenburgh graduated Summa Cum Laude from Syracuse University and has worked
as an artist and illustrator ever since. This is the ninth book she has illustrated for Flyleaf Publishing.

A Book to Remember™
Published by Flyleaf Publishing

For orders or information, contact us at **(800) 449-7006**.
Please visit our website at **www.flyleafpublishing.com**

Eighth Edition 2/20
Library of Congress Catalog Card Number: 2008937542
ISBN-13: 978-1-60541-014-2
Printed and bound in the USA at Worzalla Publishing, Stevens Point, WI.

For my mom, who introduced me to the beauty of a Luna moth when I was eight years old.

LAS

Celebrating all the little miracles of life!

CV

A tiny Luna moth egg sits on a walnut leaf.
The egg is as big as the tip of a pen.

2

The tiny egg sits on the leaf for two weeks.
Finally, a little caterpillar pops from the egg.

The caterpillar's diet is leaves from trees and plants.
The caterpillar eats and eats.

The tiny caterpillar is able to eat up to two walnut leaves every day!

6

As the caterpillar develops, or gets bigger, its skin splits. The caterpillar wiggles from the split skin.

The caterpillar has a new and bigger skin to grow into.

When the caterpillar is four weeks old,
its body will be fully developed.

At this step in its development,
the caterpillar uses its silk to spin a cocoon.
The silk is like the silk of a spider's web.

The caterpillar is in the cocoon for two to three weeks.

But in the cocoon the caterpillar is not resting....
The caterpillar is transforming itself.

At this step in its development,
the caterpillar is called a pupa.

A pupa is the step in development between
being a caterpillar and a moth.

14

Finally, the cocoon opens. A Luna moth wiggles from it.

When the Luna moth exits the cocoon,
its body is big and its wings are small and soft.

The Luna moth's wings have to open
and fill with fluid from the moth's body.

The fluid fills up and expands the moth's wings.

The Luna moth rests on a tree trunk until the evening. This will enable her new wings to dry and stiffen.

20

Finally, she lifts up on her fantastic wings
and begins a hunt for a mate.

And after meeting her mate,
the Luna moth will spend one week
dropping tiny eggs onto walnut leaves...

 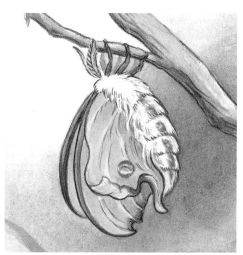 

Prerequisite Skills

Single consonants and short vowels
Final double consonants **ff**, **gg**, **ll**, **nn**, **ss**, **tt**, **zz**
Consonant /k/ **ck**
/ng/ **n[k]**
Consonant digraphs /ng/ **ng**, /th/ **th**, /hw/ **wh**
Schwa /ə/ **a**, **e**, **i**, **o**, **u**
Long /ē/ **ee**, **y**
r-Controlled /ûr/ **er**
/ô/ **al**, **all**
/ul/ **le**
/d/ or /t/ **–ed**

Target Letter-Sound Correspondence

Long /ā/ sound spelled **a**

a
able
enable

Target Letter-Sound Correspondence

Long /ē/ sound spelled **e**

be	developed
begins	development
being	develops
between	

Target Letter-Sound Correspondence

Long /ī/ sound spelled **i**

diet	spider's
finally	tiny

Target Letter-Sound Correspondence

Long /ō/ sound spelled **o**

open
opens

Target Letter-Sound Correspondences

Long /ū/ and long /o͞o/ sounds spelled **u**

fluid
Luna
pupa

High-Frequency Puzzle Words

are	into
day	like
eat	new
eats	of
every	one
for	or
four	she
from	to
fully	two
grow	uses
have	

Decodable Words

after	gets	pen	this
and	has	plants	three
as	her	pops	tip
at	hunt	resting	tree
big	in	rests	trees
bigger	is	silk	trunk
body	it	sits	until
but	its	skin	up
called	itself	small	walnut
dropping	lifts	soft	web
egg	little	spend	week
eggs	meeting	spin	weeks
exits	Moth	split	when
expands	Moth's	splits	wiggles
fantastic	not	step	will
fill	old	stiffen	wings
fills	on	the	with

Story Puzzle Words

caterpillar	leaf
caterpillar's	leaves
cocoon	mate
dry	onto
evening	transforming